# BEHIND TI
# I HAVE LEARN                                    ⌡
# TO PRAY

## BY

## RICHARD McILKENNY

PUBLISHED BY:

PAX CHRISTI (Britain)

THE CAMPAIGN FOR THE BIRMINGHAM 6

ROYALTIES from the sale of this book will go to LISIEUX HOUSE.
Richard knows the community through their visits to Wormwood Scrubs.

ISBN 1 87 23 70 00 4

"Parade of innocence"
Dublin. June 1990.
Cover and centre photographs by
Denis Mortell (N.U.J.)
Dublin Tel: 710332

Typeset & Printed by Dudley Print 081-980 4001

DESIGNED BY Henry Bran (PRAXIS)

# CONTENTS

# BEHIND THE BARS
# I HAVE LEARNED AGAIN
# TO PRAY

## BY

## INTRODUCTION

These poems written by Dick McIlkenny, are incredible evidence of human resilience. There would have been every justification, in the author, for hatred, bitterness and despair in the "community of sorrow" where he is now unjustly placed.

Nevertheless these poems are alive with religious faith and the long and hopeful view. I salute an ordinary man who despite years of injustice has risen astonishingly above the tragic circumstances of his life.

*Bruce Kent*

## DEDICATION

This book is dedicated to all those I love.

To the thousands of people around the world who have given their support over the years to our struggle for justice, especially in their letters many of which I have been as yet unable to answer, a daunting task with the continuing flow of mail such as I and my friends received but one that I will gladly continue to struggle with.

A special dedication to Sr. Kathryn Keigher, it was her insistence that a verse to go with a cover I designed for her come not from scripture but from out of my head that brought this collection of poems into being.

My sincere thanks to Bruce Kent for his kind words and his dedication to justice and peace, a man I am proud to call friend.

Prayer is the gateway to peace and it is my hope that all who read this book will enter this gateway frequently that the hypocrisy, oppression and injustice that has enveloped the world be changed into the joy and peace that can come only from a loving God.

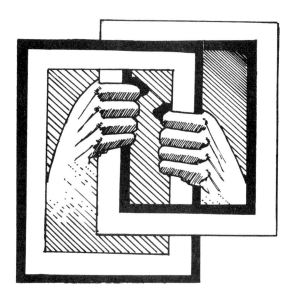

# POEMS...
## Poemas...

## BEHIND THE BARS...

Behind the bars
within my cell
I have learned again to pray.

For in despair I did forget
and from God I turned away.

But he never turned away from me
and through those that I hold dear
he shone his healing light of love
and caused my mind to clear.

Now, daily in my cell I pray
and give praise to God above
for showing me the wonders
of his true eternal love.

## DETRAS DE LOS BARROTES...

Detrás de los barrotes
dentro de mi celda
he aprendido nuevamente a orar.

Ya que en desesperación me olvidé
y de Dios me alejé.

Pero El nunca se alejé de mí
y por medio de aquellos a los que estimo
me mostró su luz sanadora de amor
y causó que mi mente se iluminara.

Hoy, oro diariamente en mi celda
y alabo a Dios en lo alto
por mostrarme las maravillas
de su verdadero y eterno amor.

## EACH MORNING I AWAKE...

Each morning I awake Lord
I give you thanks and praise
for adding yet another,
to my span of days.

In times of anger and frustration Lord
you have given me your peace
and filled me with your love and joy
that I pray
will never cease.

Through the good days
and the bad days Lord
you have carried me along
and put in my heart your patience
and on my lips your song.

Continue Lord to guide me
along the path
that is straight and narrow
that behind these prison bars
I will never cause you sorrow.

Bless me Lord
to say and do
all things
for your name's sake
and to grow stronger
in my prayers and praise
each morning I awake.

## CADA MAÑANA AL DESPERTAR...

Cada mañana al despertar Señor
te doy gracias y alabanzas
por agregar aún más
el espacio de mis días.

En tiempos de cólera y frustración Señor
me has dado tu paz
y me has llenado con tu amor y alegría
por la cual oro
para que nunca me falte.

Atraves de los días buenos
y los días malos Señor
tú me has cargado
y has puesto en mi corazón tu paciencia
y en mis labios tu canción.

Continua Señor guiandome
a lo largo del camino
que es recto y angosto
que detrás de estos barrotes de la prisión
yo nunca te cause dolor.

Bendíceme Señor
para decir y hacer
todas las cosas
por el bien de tu nombre
y para crecer fuerte
en mis oraciones y alabanzas
cada mañada al despertar.

## AS OUTCASTS OF SOCIETY...

As outcasts of society
locked up in prisons bare
the Eucharist Lord
is the gift to us
in which we all can share.

In communion Lord
we are made as one by you
our God and gracious king
by your sacrifice you give us life
and we in joy,
your praises sing.

No longer are we outcasts
for in you we realise
that to love and trust
in your sweet word
will lead to paradise.

We are a community of sorrow
now hope sets our hearts
aflame
by the Eucharist
you have changed us Lord
to a community of your name.

## COMO VAGABUNDOS DE LA SOCIEDAD...

Como vagabundos de la sociedad
encerrados en la soledad de la prisión
la Eucaristía Señor
es el dón para nosotros
en el cual todos podemos compartir.

En comunión Señor
somos hechos uno por tí
Dios nuestro y grandioso Rey
por tú sacrificio
nos has dado vida
y nosotros en alegría
cantamos tus alabanzas.

Ya no somos vagabundos
porque en tí nos damos cuenta
que amar y confiar
en tu dulce palabra
nos llevará al paraiso.

Somos una comunidad de dolor.
y la esperanza enciende nuestro corazón
en llamas
con la Eucaristía
tú nos has cambiado Señor
a una comunidad de tu nombre.

## OUTSIDE THE CELL...

Outside the cell
in view of all
a cheery smile
a hearty call.

Behind the door
where no one can see
sighs and tears most bitter.

No joy or peace here can be found,
no trust, no love.
nor true knowledge of the Lord

Just grief and sorrow all around
and mockery of his word.

They do not know,
have not been taught of the love
and joy that can be theirs
if they would only turn to God
with their heartaches and their cares.

So please send your Holy Spirit, Lord
and open up our minds
that our time here may not be wasted
but with your words entwined.

## AFUERA DE LA CELDA...

Afuera de la celda
en vista de todo
una alegre sonrisa
un llamado sincero.

Detrás de la puerta
en donde nadie puede ver
los suspiros y llantos más amargos.

Aquí no se puede encontrar la alegría,
ni la paz, ni la confianza, ni el amor
ni el verdadero conocimiento del Señor.

Solo aflicción y dolor por todo el rededor
y burla de su palabra.

Ellos no saben,
nunca se les ha enseñado del amor
y felicidad que puede ser de ellos
si solo cambiaran hacia Dios
con sus angustias y sus inquietudes.

Por favor manda tu Espíritu Santo, Señor
y abre nuestras mentes
para que nuestro tiempo aquí no sea desperdiciado
sino para ser tejidos en tus palabras.

## *YOU SUFFERED LORD...*

You suffered Lord
that we should live
free from the bonds of sin.

You died for us,
then rose again
that we might enter in
to the heavenly place prepared for us
amidst angelic hosts.

Ascension day you did return
to your father's home of grace
and sent to us the Holy Ghost
to guide us in your place.

Now we who live in prison Lord
have heard your gracious song
and we pray each day
that the "comforter"
will guide our lives along
the lanes and pathways
you did set,
the roadways you did trod.

That we at last could come to you
our sweet and loving God.

## TU SUFRISTES SEÑOR...

Tú sufristes Señor
para que nosotros vivieramos
libres de las cadenas del pecado.

Tú moristes por nosotros
luego resucitastes
para que pudieramos entrar
al lugar celestial preparado para nosotros
entre huestes angelicales.

En el día de ascensión regresastes
al hogar bendito de tu padre
y mandastes para nosotros tu Espiritu Santo
para guiarnos en tu lugar.

Ahora Señor, los que vivimos en prisión
hemos escuchado tu bendita canción
y oramos cada día
para que el "consolador"
guíe nuestras vidas
a lo largo de los caminos y senderos
que pusistes,
de las calles que caminastes.

Para que al final podamos venir a tí
nuestro dulce y amoroso Dios.

## *YOU TAUGHT US HOW TO PRAY LORD...*

You taught us how to pray Lord
but sometimes we forget
as our minds we allow to wander
and on earthly things they set.

Inside each joyless prison cell
thoughts of you do scatter
as forlorn and lonely inmates
dwell on things that do not matter.

So please Lord
in your mercy
send your Holy Spirit
to each cell
and turn our minds again Lord
on your loving heart to dwell.

Teach us again to pray Lord
with happiness and love
that we may sing our praises
to you Lord in heaven above.

## TU NOS ENSEÑASTES A ORAR SEÑOR...

Tú nos enseñastes a orar Señor
pero algunas veces nos olvidamos
mientras permitimos que nuestras mentes vagen
y se detengan en cosas terrenales.

Dentro de cada triste celda en la prisión
pensamientos de tí se esparcen
ya que los prisioneros desamparados y solos
viven en cosas que no importan.

Así que por favor Señor
en tu misericordia
manda tu Espiritu Santo
a cada celda
y vuelve nuestras mentes nuevamente Señor
a vivir en tu amoroso corazón.

Enséñanos nuevamente a orar Señor
con felicidad y amor
para que podamos cantar nuestras alabanzas
a tí Señor en lo alto del cielo.

## PEACE AND GOOD WILL LORD...

"Peace and Good Will" Lord
your angels sang
as they came down from the stars
but it seems to have stopped short Lord
outside the prison bars.

So please Lord
send them onward
that their message they may tell
to every sad and lonely heart
inside each prison cell

Fill us all with love and joy Lord
so that on Christmas night we too
may sing out with your angels
our praises and love for you.

## PAZ Y BUENA VOLUNTAD SEÑOR...

"Paz y Buena Voluntad" Señor
tus angeles cantaban
mientras bajaban de las estrellas
pero parecen haberse detenido antes Señor
afuera de los barrotes de la celda.

Por favor Señor
mandalos
para que su mensaje puedan decir
a cada triste y solitario corazón
dentro de cada celda en la prisión.

Llenanos a todos con amor y alegría Señor
para que en la noche de Navidad nosotros también
podamos cantar con tus angeles
nuestras alabanzas y amor para tí.

## YOU WERE A PRISONER IN ME LORD...

You were a prisoner in me Lord
and I could not set you free
for behind these prison bars
I looked with eyes that could not see
the sorrow and the heartache
the bewilderment and the shame
that exist here all around me
in ignorance of your name.

I had forgotten you were there Lord
lying deep within my soul
just waiting for the moment
when you could make me whole.
You took the scales from off my eyes Lord
and filled me with your love
through those that you did bring to me
like angels from above.

Now I thank you Lord
with all my heart
and pray that I too might be used
to bring your word to others
so that from their bonds they might be loosed.

Within these walls and bars Lord
men live in loneliness and shame
so please Lord
use me to help them
for the glory of your name.

## TU ESTABAS PRESO EN MI SEÑOR...

Tú estabas preso en mí Señor
y no te podía liberar
ya que detrás de estos barrotes de la prisión
miraba con ojos que no podían ver
la tristesa y la angustia,
la confusión y la pena
que existe aquí a mi alrededor
en ignorancia de tu nombre.

Había olvidado que estabas allí Señor
en lo profundo dentro de mi alma
esperando solamente el momento
a que tú me hicieras completamente.
Tú quitastes las escamas de mis ojos Señor
y me llenastes con tu amor
por medio de aquellos que trajistes a mí
como angeles de lo alto.

Ahora te agradezco Señor
con todo mi corazón
y oro de que yo también sea usado
para llevar tu palabra a otros
para que de sus cadenas sean liberados.

Dentro de estas paredes y barrotes Señor
los hombres viven en soledad y pena
por favor Señor
usame para ayudarle a ellos
por la gloria de tu nombre.

## AS YOU LOOK DOWN...

As you look down
on this sad world Lord
forgive us all our sins
of indifference and neglect
and for the state that it's now in.

In our selfishness Lord
we turned away
from the beauty of your hands
the birds, the beasts
and flowers with which
you graced our lands.

We have ravished Lord
and plundered
this globe you did create
not for need but
because of greed
of envy and of hate.

Look down
on this sad world Lord
and do forgive us what we have done
that we may rebuild on
what you gave.

The life of your only son.

## *MIENTRAS TU VES HACIA ABAJO...*

Mientras tú ves hacia abajo
sobre este triste mundo Señor
perdona todos nuestros pecados
de indiferencia y negligencia
y por el estado en el cual está ahora.

En nuestro egoismo Señor
nos hemos apartado
de la belleza de tus manos
las aves, las bestias
y las flores con las cuales
distes gracia a nuestras tierras.

Hemos raptado Señor
y saqueado
este globo que tú has creado
no por necesidad sino
por avaricia
de envidia y odio.

Mira hacia abajo
sobre este mundo triste Señor
y perdónanos lo que hemos hecho
para que reconstruyamos
lo que nos distes.

La vida de tu único hijo.

## BEHIND THESE PRISON BARS...

Behind these prison bars
there was never much to see
until you came into my heart Lord
and reawakened me.

Now I see you all around me
in the suffering and shame
in the eyes of those who do not know
the blessings of your name.

Your lost sheep are all here Lord
in the sadness and despair
and I pray you Lord
give me the grace
to bring them back into your care.

They are wandering lost and lonely
and cannot see your love
so please Lord
help me help them
with your guidance
from above.

## DETRAS DE LOS BARROTES DE LA PRISION...

Detrás de los barrotes de la prisión
nunca había mucho que ver
hasta que tú venistes a mi corazón Señor
y nuevamente me despertastes.

Ahora te veo por todo mi alrededor
en el sufrimiento y en la pena
en los ojos de los que no conocen
las bendiciones de tu nombre.

Tus ovejas perdidas estan todas aquí Señor
en tristesa y desesperación
y yo te pido a tí Señor
dame tu gracia
para traerlos de nuevo a tus cuidados.

Ellos vagan perdidos y solos
y no pueden ver tu amor
por favor Señor
ayudame para ayudarle a ellos
con tu dirección
desde lo alto.

## IN LONELINESS AND HEARTACHE...

In loneliness and heartache
in sadness and despair
I bend my knee
to you Lord
in humility and prayer.

You came to me
in my darkest hour
and helped me
overcome my pain
you filled me with your joy and peace
and made me to live again.

So, whatever I may do Lord
or wherever I may be
I will give thanks
and praise to you Lord
upon my bended knee.

## EN SOLEDAD Y ANGUSTIA...

En soledad y angustia,
en tristeza y desesperación
doblo mis rodillas
a tí Señor
en humildad y oración.

Tú venístes a mí
en mi hora más oscura
y me ayudastes
a sobrepasar mi dolor
tú me llenastes con tu felicidad y paz
y me has hecho vivir nuevamente.

Así, lo que sea que yo haga Señor
o donde sea que esté
daré gracias
y alabanzas a tí Señor
incado en mis rodillas.

## THE FLAMES OF INNOCENCE...

The flames of innocence
burn bright against the darkness
of oppression and the pillars
of bigotry and hatred
wrapped in foul obsession
cringe in fear
of truth's bright beams of light.

For justice,
is once again
emerging from where she
had been banned
to the singing of the people's
as they march together
hand in hand
with "FREEDOM FOR THE INNOCENTS"
as their song
throughout the land.

## LAS LLAMAS DE LA INOCENCIA...

Las llamas de la inocencia
alumbran brillantes contra la oscuridad
de la opresión y los pilares
de la intolerancia y el odio
envueltos en la sucia obsesión
encogido en miedo
por los rayos de la verdad de luz brillante.

Por la justicia,
emergen nuevamente desde donde ella
había sido prohibida
hasta el cantó del pueblo
mientras marchan juntos
mano a mano
con "LIBERTAD PARA LOS INOCENTES"
como su canción
atraves de la tierra.

## WHAT PRICE...

What price, justice for the innocents
locked up in prison cells.

What price, respect and peace of mind
for those who know and will not tell.

What price, the horror of the beatings,
the torture and the cries
of honest men who in terror signed
perverted statements filled with lies.

What price, hunger and deprivation,
threats with guns and growling dogs
of minds now blank and wandering
as if lost within a fog.

What price, the cries of wives and children
of families torn apart
whose moans and wails of anguish
come from deeply wounded hearts.

What price, the long lost years
filled with loneliness and pain
and the longing to be held
in loving arms again.

## QUE PRECIO...

Qué precio, justicia para los inocentes
encerrados en las celdas de la prisión.

Que precio, respeto y paz mental
para aquellos que saben y no dirán.

Qué precio, el horror de los golpes,
la tortura y los llantos
de hombres honestos quienes aterrorizados firmaron
declaraciones pervertidas llenas de mentiras.

Qué precio, hambre y deprivación
amenazas con armas y perros gruñentes
de mentes ahora vacias y vagas
como perdidas en la neblina.

Qué precio, los llantos de esposas y niños.
de familias hechas pedazos
cuyos lamentos y gemidos de angustia
vienen profundamente desde los corazones heridos.

Qué precio, los largos años perdidos
llenos de soledad y dolor
y el deseo de ser tomado nuevamente
en brazos amorosos.

What price, the lost love
and joy of children
all now fully grown.
Left without a father
now with children of their own.

What price, what price!!

What price, for honesty and truthfulness
for dignity and pride restored
for the innocents to be set free
exonerated and recompensed
to rejoin society once more.

Qué precio, el amor perdido
y la alegría de los niños
ya todos crecidos.
Dejados sin padre
y ahora con sus propios hijos.

¡¡Qué precio, qué precio!!

Qué precio, por honestidad y verdad,
por dignidad y por el orgullo restaurado,
para que los inocentes que sean libres
disculpados y recompensados
para reunirse a la sociedad una vez más.

## MORNING DEAR...

—Morning dear.

The neighbour calls
as she passes on her way.

—Is there anything you need
while I'm shopping out today?
Mary Jane will be along to clean,
and Agnes will cook dinner.
You like her cakes with cream?...

...No dear, we are neighbours
and as such, we care a lot.
No need for you to fuss,
So just sit back there and relax
and leave the rest to us.

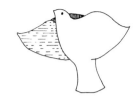

## BUENOS DIAS QUERIDA...

—Buenos días querida.

La vecina llama
mientras pasa de camino.

—¿Hay algo que usted necesite
mientras ando de compras ahora?
Mary Jane vendré a limpiar,
y Agnes cocinará la cena.
—¿A usted le gustan sus pastelitos con crema?...

...No querida, somos vecinas
y como tales, les queremos mucho.
No hay necesidad de que se moleste,
así es que sientese allí y relajese
y deje el resto a nosotros.

## EMBRYO...

We have legalised
your death
you're not really
one of us
with your handicap
you won't fit in
so, don't kick up a fuss
you are good just for experiments
then in the bin
with all the rest
but for fourteen days
you belong to us
until we have finished
all our tests
stiff upper lip
and all that rot
no use to cry or frown
it doesn't matter
that you might be
another Christy Brown.

*EMBRION...*

Hemos legalizado
tu muerte
verdaderamente no eres
uno de nosotros
con tus incapacidades
tú no caberas
así es que no hagas problemas
tú eres bueno solo para los experimentos
luego a la basura
con todo el resto
pero por catorce días
tú nos perteneces
hasta que terminemos
todos nuestros examenes
labio superior tieso
y toda esa pudrición
no vale llorar o fruncir la frente
no importa
que tú seas
otro Christy Brown.

## I'LL GIVE UP FAGS TOMORROW LORD...

I'll give up fags tomorrow Lord
when I've finished off this snout.

I know I promised last week
but I had lent some out
to friends who didn't have none.

Now they've paid me back
some of what I'd lent
so tomorrow I'm all yours Lord
well, except maybe "five per cent."

Five per cent's not much Lord
not when measured by our scales
especially when I'm locked up
inside this lousy jail.

Have I upset you someway Lord?
cause I'm feeling very rough
I got out of bed this morning
and I got an awful cough
I made me a roll up
and thought, "I'll have a smoke"
but every time I took a puff
dear God,
I nearly choked.

I'll tell the others
not to bother
about the snout I've lent
then you can have me all Lord
including the "five per cent."

## *DEJARE EL CIGARRILLO MAÑANA SEÑOR...*

Dejaré el cigarrillo mañana Señor
cuando me haya dejado de fumar este.

Sé que lo prometí la semana pasada
pero había prestado algunos
a amigos que no tenían ninguno.

Ahora ellos me han pagado de regreso
algunos de los que había prestado
así es que mañana seré todo tuyo Señor
bueno, excepto talvez el "cinco por ciento."

Cinco por ciento no es mucho Señor
no cuando es medido por nuestras balanzas
especialmente cuando estoy encerrado
en esta asquerosa celda.

¿Te he enojado en alguna forma Señor?
pues me siento muy mal
me levante de la cama esta mañana
y tenía una terrible tos
y pensé, "fumarme uno"
pero cada vez que tomaba una bocanada
hay Dios mio,
casi me ahogo.

Yo les digo a los otros
que no se preocupen
por los cigarrilos que he prestado
así tú puedes tenerme todo Señor
incluyendo el "cinco por ciento."

*I THANK YOU LORD...*

I thank you Lord of light and love
for the guidance
you have given me from heaven up above.
In the dark years
of my life Lord
when I stumbled
and did fall
you shone your beams
of kindness and compassion in answer to my call
with your love came understanding
and my faith has grown anew.

So by your grace
my Lord of light and love
I pledge my will to you.

## TE AGRADEZCO SEÑOR...

Te agradezco Señor de luz y amor
por la guía
que me has dado desde lo alto del cielo.
En los años oscuros
de mi vida Señor
cuando tropecé
y caí
tú mostrastes tus rayos
de amabilidad y compación en respuesta a mi llamado
con tu amor vino el entendimiento
y mi amor a crecido nuevamente.

Así por tu gracia
mi Señor de luz y amor
empeño mi voluntad a tí.

## REMEMBER THOSE IN PRISON...

Remember those in prison
each time
you kneel in prayer
and ask the Lord
to bless
and heal the souls
that sadly languish there.

Behind prison bars
life
can be dreary and forlorn
and the hours
can pass so slowly
between each sunset
and each morn.

So remember those in prison
when you pray to God above
that the sadness
and the longing there
may be healed
by his sweet love.

## RECUERDA A LOS QUE ESTAN EN PRISION...

Recuerda a los que están en prisión
cada vez
que te inques en oración
y pidele al Señor
que bendiga
y sane las almas
que tristemente languidecen ahí.

Detrás de los barrotes de la prisión
la vida
puede ser triste y desamparada
y las horas
pueden pasar tan despacio
entre cada atardecer
y cada mañana.

Así que recuerda a los que estan en prisión
cuando ores a Dios en lo alto
que la tristeza
y el anhelo en ese lugar
pueda ser sanado
por su dulce amor.

## *A KNOCK UPON THE DOOR LORD...*

A knock upon the door Lord
a whisper low and clear.

—Will you pray for me?

I don't know how
came softly to my ear
I answered,

—Yes, most certainly.

And went on bended knee
then as I pray for one sad friend
I hoped, someone prayed for me.

For though I do pray often
and in other ways give praise
I know that each and every day
I fail in other ways.

Sadly there are many men in prison
who were never taught to pray.

## UN TOQUE SOBRE LA PUERTA SEÑOR...

Un toque sobre la puerta Señor
un susurro suave y claro.

—¿Puedes orar por mí?

Yo no sé como llegó
suavemente a mi oido
y contesté,

—Sí, claro que si.

Y caí de rodillas
y mientras oraba por un amigo triste
espero, que alguien haya orado por mí.

Porque aunque yo oro seguido
y en otras formas doy alabanza
sé que cada y todos los días
falló en otras cosas.

Tristemente hay muchos hombres en prición
a quienes nunca se les enseñó a orar.

Now they feel their need for you Lord
but don't know what to say
I will do my best
in any way I can
but I will need help also
for I too am just a man.

So let your light
shine on this prison Lord
and bless us one and all
that daily we may pray as one
In answer to your call.

Ahora sienten la necesidad por tí Señor
pero no saben que decir
yo haré lo mejor
en cualquier forma que pueda
pero también necesitaré ayuda
ya que también yo solo soy un hombre.

Así es que deja tu luz
brillar sobre esta prisión Señor
y bendícenos a uno y a todos
para que a diario oremos como uno
en respuesta a tu llamado.

## YOUR WORD OF LIFE...

Your word of life
you gave to us
to guide us
on our way.

Your grace, this word
does keep us in
as we travel through
each day.

Your word, your grace,
your love strengthens us
in all our strife
and we thank you Lord
of heaven and earth
for giving us
your word of life.

## TU PALABRA DE VIDA...

Tu palabra de vida
nos distes
para guiarnos
en nuestro camino.

Tu gracia, tu palabra
nos mantenga
mientras viajamos atravez
de cada día.

Tu palabra, tu gracia,
tu amor, nos fortalezca
en todas nuestras contiendas
y te agradecemos Señor
del cielo y la tierra
por darnos
tu palabra de vida.

## EACH DAY FROM EARLY MORN...

Each day from early morn
they murder and condemn
God's children yet unborn
almost every fifteen minutes
an unborn child is slain
and the innocent Christ child
bleeds profusely
over rubbish bins
filled with dead.

With each death
he is once more crucified
and cries to us in agony
to assault the gates of heaven
with prayers to set him free
for it is within our hearts
he lives
and we daily cause him pain
by ignoring injustice
and abortion
carried out again and again.

So on our knees
before our God
we must beg him
to forgive
and that through his grace
put in our hearts
the unborn child
might live.

## CADA DIA DESDE MUY DE MAÑANA...

Cada día desde muy de mañana
ellos asesinan y condenan
a los hijos de Dios aún sin nacer
casi cada quince minutos
un niño aún sin nacer es muerto
y el niño Cristo inocente
sangra profusamente
sobre los basureros
llenos de muertos.

Con cada muerte
él es crucificado una vez más
y nos llora en agonía
para asaltar los portones del cielo
con oraciones para liberarlo
porque es dentro de nuestro corazón
en donde vive
y diariamente le causamos dolor
ignorando las injusticias y la aborción
llevadas a cabo una y otra vez.

Así, de rodillas ante nuestro Dios
debemos rogarle que perdone
y que atraves de su gracia
ponga en nuestros corazones
el niño que no ha nacido para que viva.

## *AS EACH DAY COMES TO AN END...*

As each day comes to an end Lord
I give thanks and praise to you
for giving me the strength and grace
to carry on and see it through.

Behind bars it is not easy Lord
away from family and friends
and without your grace and blessings
days seem to have no end.

It was hard but I have learned Lord
to put my trust in you
and you in turn have blessed me greatly
with love and patience strong and true.

So as each day comes to an end
to you my Lord my voice I raise
in prayers of joyful thanks
and words of heartfelt praise.

## *CUANDO CADA DIA LLEGA A SU FINAL...*

Cuando cada día llega a su final Señor
doy gracias y alabanzas a tí
por darme la fuerza y la bendición
para continuar y verlo pasar.

Detrás de los barrotes no es facil Señor
lejos de la familia y amigos
y sin tu gracia y bendiciones
los días parecen no tener final.

Ha sido duro pero he aprendido Señor
a poner mi confianza en tí
y tú, en turnos me has bendecido grandemente
con amor y paciencia fuerte y verdadera.

Así, mientras cada día llega a su final
a tí mi Señor levanto mi voz
en oraciones de agradecimientos alegres
y palabras de alabanza que siente el corazón.

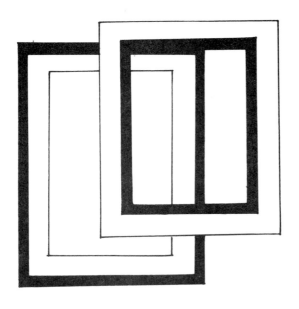

## LISIEUX HOUSE

50 Birmingham Road
Sutton Coldfield
West Midlands B72 1QJ

A COMMUNITY HOME SHARED WITH MEN AND WOMEN
WHO HAVE A MENTAL HANDICAP

Established by the LISIEUX TRUST
A Registered Charity (No 292517)

The Lisieux Trust was formed in 1983 gathering together a group of
Christian people who saw their vision become a reality when Lisieux
House was opened in September 1986. Seven people all with special
needs share their lives with a loving family, care assistants and
supportive volunteers. All those living at the House have now grown
into one family.

The House is situated in the centre of Sutton Coldfield and is
supported by the wider community. People help in many ways;
some invite members into their homes for meals, week-ends or
holidays while others help by raising funds for our continuing and
expanding work. Everyone is aware that help will always be needed
from local churches and from professional people with their special
skills.

At Lisieux House all share household chores as everyone is
encouraged to acquire and develop skills which will allow a degree
of independence for example shopping, cooking, washing and
ironing. Everyone has some skills which they can use to help the rest
of the family.

Meal times are not fixed but everyone tries to eat together: even those
rushing out to work manage to sit down to breakfast and there is
usually a full house for supper.

The daytime routine is varied as members of the family attend different places of work and training centres. These include basic education, computing, gardening, craft and woodwork which allow for greater opportunity for integration into the local community and maybe one day - a job!

Lisieux House is registered as a Charitable Trust. Trustees undertake to be responsible for funding the finance for all capital costs. The daily expenses of the community are met by D.H.S.S. allowances.

Early in 1988 the opportunity arose to purchase a further property adjacent to Lisieux House. This will enable the Trust to expand its work.

The aim is to provide homes for people with a mental handicap in a Christian atmosphere for the rest of their lives.

They believe that this is important. They wish their mentally handicapped brothers and sisters to live as full a life as possible and to continue sharing with us their precious gifts which our society so badly needs.

Adults with special needs will always be welcome irrespective of religion, race, colour or creed.

Enquiries to:
Miss P. Lucas
Lisieux House
47 Sutton Court
Little Sutton Lane
Sutton Coldfield B75 6SE

## LONDON CAMPAIGN FOR THE BIRMINGHAM 6

Is part of the national campaign body which seeks the freedom and complete exoneration of the six men.

Birmingham Six Group
1, Orleston Road
London NW1

c/o Sandy Boyer
606 45th Street Brooklyn
New York 11220
U.S.A.
Tel: 718-436-4770

c/o Kathy Lisowski
70 Pearl Street No 1-214
Brookline MA, 02146
U.S.A.
Tel: 617-738-6583

c/o Roger Poirier
144 Fairmount Street
San Francisco, CA 94131
U.S.A.
Tel: 415-821-4069

The Irish Commission for Prisoners Overseas,
The Bishops' Commission for Emigrants
57 Parnell Square
Dublin 1
Tel: 722511

## PAX CHRISTI
9 Henry Road, London N4 2LH
Tel:081-800 4612

Is an International Peace Organisation. The British section approached the newly appointed Cardinal Hume in 1977 to look at the case of the Guildford 4, Birmingham 6 and Maguire 7: especially expressing concern for Giuseppe Conlon who was to die in prison in 1980.


## MOVEMENT FOR FAITH AND JUSTICE TODAY
2 Tynemouth Street, Fulham SW6 2QT
Tel: 071-736 7624

A group of people who meet and reflect together integrating life and gospel concerns in basic community style. There are groups who meet together over specialist concerns. This connection has been involved in inspiring an evening prayer group at "The Scrubs" over many years.


## SOCIETY FOR THE PROTECTION OF THE UNBORN CHILD
7 Tuston Street, London SW1
Tel: 071-222 5845

Is a political campaigning organisation working through its membership throughout society. It also provides an educational service. It has a limited involvement in counselling and it is one organisation of which Richard is a member.


## PRO-LIFERS FOR PEACE
11 Ruskin Court, Champion Hill
London SE5 8AH

Is a national organisation which seeks non-violent solutions to human problems and campaigns against abortion and nuclear weapons. This belief they see as a consistent pro-life and pro-peace position.